D0979446

What's the Deal with Retirement Communities?

Brad C. Breeding

Table of Contents

Introduction

According to the U.S. Census Bureau there are over 12 million people in the United States between the ages of sixty-five and sixty-nine[1]– and that number continues to grow as approximately 10,000 people celebrate their sixty-fifth birthday every day.[2] Most people in this age group are able to live independently, but that may change as they get older. Therefore, it is important to plan now for your later retirement years.

A post by an Elder Law attorney Bernard Krooks on Forbes.com in February 2011 titled *The Five Phases of Retirement Planning* describes "mid-retirement" as the phase that "begins at age seventy and lasts as long as you are able-bodied and high-functioning." Krooks then states, "Despite your good health, begin looking at what steps you would like your family to take should your condition decline significantly."[3]

---

1 United States. Census Bureau. "Table 1. Population by Age and Sex: 2010." *United States Census 2010.* Washington: US Census Bureau, June 2011. Web. 12 March 2014. https://www.census.gov/population/age/data/2010comp.html

2 Cohn, D'vera and Paul Taylor, "Baby Boomers Approach 65- Glumly." *Pew Research Social and Demographic Trends.* Pew Research, 20 Dec. 2010. Web. 5 Dec. 2013.

3 Krooks, B. "The Five Phases of Retirement Living *Forbes.* Forbes,16 Feb. 2011. Web. 11 Nov. 2013.

The article describes the "late-phase" of retirement as the point when "…your health has taken a turn for the worse and there is little likelihood of it being fully restored. You require significant help to function day to day. The hope is that by this point all the planning done in prior years makes this transition as manageable and life-affirming as possible."[4]

Make a plan

Not only is the older American population growing but, as a result of advances in medicine and technology, people are living longer. A seventy-year old male in the U.S. can expect to live over fourteen more years on average while a female can expect to live over sixteen more years, but rarely without the need for some degree of long-term care services. (Of course, some will live much longer than the average.)

The possibility of a longer lifetime combined with extended long-term care necessitates the need for families to take a more proactive approach to planning for the later phases of retirement. Yet, this is an aspect of planning that is often neglected by families and financial advisors alike. Our society tends to be mostly reactive in addressing the lifestyle and health care needs that we may face in the later years of life. Families often wait until a significant health event occurs before researching options.

Usually this responsibility falls on the adult children or other family members who are forced to quickly shift into "crisis-man-agement mode" and may not have the resources, flexibility in schedule, or emotional capacity to take on such a task.

4 Centers for Medicare and Medicaid Services, *Medicare and You 2014- Official U.S. Government Medicare Handbook. http://knowledgecenter.unr.edu/help/manage/government_cite.aspx#agencycorp*

If you are approaching, or are in the "mid-retirement" phase, now is the time to plan for your later years of retirement—while you are still active and able. Otherwise, delaying these important decisions about tomorrow's needs may leave you and your loved ones facing difficult, and often costly, situations in the future. One of the more important, and complex, decisions you or your loved ones need to consider is where you will live and how your future care needs will be provided. As you read about the various retirement living choices covered in this book keep in mind that *paying for care* and *access to care* are separate issues. For instance, owning long-term care insurance will help pay for care but it does not address the other aspect of the issue—where and how your eventual care needs will be provided.

Purpose of this Book

Many people are confused by the array of choices available across the spectrum of senior living. The reality is that the term "retirement community" is often used rather generically; therefore, it is important to have a clear understanding of what to look for when researching the options.

The purpose of this book is to educate you in plain language on the different types of retirement communities. I will not attempt to cover every facet of the retirement living industry, such as a description of the capital markets for senior living development or the impact of our health care system on the senior living industry. Rather, this book is designed as a first step in the research process as you contemplate the best retirement housing choice for yourself or a loved one. My goal is for you to walk away with a basic understanding of the key differences between the various types of retirement communities and other closely related issues, thus providing you with a reference point from which to start.

Equipped with a better understanding of the retirement living landscape you will be prepared to plan for your future living needs, or those of a loved one, so that the eventual transition to the later phases of life will be, as described by Krooks, "more manageable and life-affirming."

CHAPTER 1

I Just Want to Stay in my Home. Why Consider a Retirement Community?

Studies show that nearly 90% of people over age sixty-five want to stay in their home for as long as possible, and 80% believe their current residence is where they will always live.[5]

Why do such a high number of retirees seek to stay in their home? As they say, "home is where the heart is." It is a familiar setting where people feel most comfortable, surrounded by memories that create a strong emotional connection. More importantly, staying at home is symbolic of retaining independence.

Since aging at home is the obvious alternative to moving to a retirement community, I want to cover some of the important implications of this choice so you will have a point of comparison against the various types of retirement communities that I will describe in the coming chapters.

---

5 National Conference of State Legislatures and AARP Public Policy Institute, *Aging in Place: A State Survey of Livability Policies and Practices* (Washington, DC: NCSL, and Washington, DC: AARP, 2011).

Although aging at home is the preferred choice for many, it can present a number of challenges during the "late-phase" of retirement that are often not anticipated and can cause a great deal of stress on families. It should be noted that highly innovative technology is being developed every day to help older Americans age more safely and comfortably in their homes. Much of this technology can even be utilized by residents living within retirement communities. Yet, there will always be certain obstacles associated with aging at home that cannot be overcome by technology alone.

A growing concern about the elderly living at home was highlighted in a 2012 Forbes Magazine article titled *The Grim Impact of Loneliness and Living Alone*, which cited studies revealing that 43% of the 1,604 study participants (average age: 71) reported feeling lonely and that "loneliness in individuals over sixty years of age appears to be associated with increased risks of functional decline and death."[6]

There are other issues to consider, many of which arise when the ability to live independently begins to diminish. In a recent article by Jane Clark of Kiplinger Magazine focusing on aging at home, Ms. Clark states, "Keeping the family house can be sensible... if you've retired your mortgage or have enough income to pay it, and if you're relatively healthy and mobile. Eventually, however, staying at home turns into "aging in place," a term that generally means you'll need help living on your own."[7]

---

6 Husten, Larry. "The Grim Impact of Loneliness and Living Alone." *Forbes.* Forbes, 8 June 2012. Web. 10 Oct. 2013.

7 Clark, J. Bennett. "The Benefits of Aging in Place." *Forbes.* Forbes, Aug. 2013. Web. 16 Oct. 2013.

Since there is really no way to know exactly what health care needs and other challenges will arise in the future, it is important to contemplate a range of scenarios. If you plan to stay in your home here are a few questions you and your family need to consider now:

- Will your home need to be modified to accommodate potential mobility challenges?

- If you live in a two-story home, is your bedroom upstairs? If so, what is your plan if you reach the point where you are no longer able to climb stairs independently or without risk of falling?

- How will you maintain your home and yard when daily physical activity becomes more challenging?

- How will you stay socially active to minimize loneliness, even when your mobility and independence declines?

- Who will provide transportation to doctors' appointments and other necessary errands if you are no longer able drive safely?

- How will someone know if you fall and cannot get up on your own?

- Who will make sure your bills are paid if your cognitive functionality begins to decline?

- Who will help you prepare meals, get dressed, and perform other activities of daily living when you are no longer physically able?

- If you require facility-based care due to an unexpected injury, such as a fall, do you know where you will go to receive such care? Do you and your family members or other support network have a plan in place for this occurrence?

- Do you have any present health conditions or illnesses that might become more difficult to manage over time, such as diabetes or chronic lower respiratory diseases? Such illnesses could present increased challenges as you seek to stay in your home.

- If you require in-home care or assistance who will manage scheduling and payments, as well as regular oversight to assure that adequate care is provided and prevent elder abuse?

As described by Clark, aging at home will almost certainly require outside assistance or care at some point. It is important to know ahead of time how such assistance will be provided. Here is a brief explanation of the various types of in-home services and supports:

Family Caregivers

A Family Caregiver is a relative, or even a good friend, of an individual who requires some degree of assisted living. They are generally thought to be unpaid for their services, though some families may make compensation arrangements. Additionally, federal financial support may be available for caregivers when the recipient of care qualifies for Medicaid. (More on Medicaid in Chapter 6) In some cases, cash benefits may be available for Family Caregivers through a long-term care policy.

Although caring for an aging parent can be rewarding in many ways, I want to emphasize that it can also take a heavy toll physically, emotionally, and financially on the caregiver. Here are a few statistics to help illustrate this point:

- There are approximately 65 million unpaid caregivers in the United States, according to data from the National Alliance for Caregiving.[8]

- The estimated economic value of unpaid caregivers is approximately $450 billion.[9]

- Between 40 % and 70 % of caregivers are significantly stressed and about half of these caregivers meet the diagnosis for major depression.[10]

- Fifty-three percent of caregivers say caregiving takes time away from friends and other family members.[11]

Professional Home Care Services & Home Health Care Providers

While the terms are similar and often used interchangeably there is an important distinction to be made between Home Care Service Providers and Home Health Care Providers. Home Care Service Providers deliver *non-medical* services in the home, i.e. assistance with Activities of Daily Living (ADLs) and Instrumental Activities of Daily Living (IADLs), which I will describe in the next chapter. Some Home Care

8 National Alliance of Caregiving (NAC) and AARP, *Caregiving in the U.S.- Executive Summary* p., 4 .(Bethesda, MD: NAC, and Washington, DC: AARP, 2009).

9 L. Feinberg, S.C. Reinhard, A. Houser, and R. Choula. *Valuing the Invaluable: 2011 Update- The Growing Contributions and Costs of Family Caregiving.* (Washington, DC: AARP Public Policy Institute, 2011).

10 Ratini, Melinda. "Caregiver Care: Managing Stress, Depression." *WebMD.* WebMd, 1 July, 2013. Web. 12 Sept. 2014. http://www.webmd.com/palliative-care/features/caregiver-care-managing-stress-depression

11 National Alliance of Caregiving (NAC) and AARP, *Caregiving in the U.S.- Executive Summary.* p.,16 (Bethesda, MD: NAC, and Washington, DC: AARP, 2009).

Service Providers are hired simply to provide companionship. Home Care Service Providers typically are not required to be licensed by the state(s) in which they operate but would be if they accept Medicare or Medicaid reimbursements.

Home Health Care Providers, on the other hand, deliver *medically-oriented* care. Providers of home health care are licensed by the state as licensed practical nurses or therapists and often work for home health care agencies, public health care departments, or hospitals. Services may include skilled nursing care, physical therapy, occupational therapy, and speech therapy. Many home health care agencies also provide non-medical assisted living services.

CHAPTER 2

What Is a Retirement Community and How Can I Distinguish One Type from Another?

Retirement communities are not all created equal. The services offered and the extent to which they address the challenges of the "late-phase" of retirement varies from one community to another. Yet, one characteristic that retirement communities have in common is a minimum age requirement. This is why you will sometimes hear retirement communities described as "age 55+ communities." You may also hear them described as "age-restricted" or "age-qualified" communities.

Although discrimination in housing is prohibited in the United States, there is an exception for age. The Housing for Older Persons Act of 1995 (HOPA) allows communities to restrict ownership to older individuals if either of the following requirements is met:

- All of the occupants of the community are age sixty-two or older, or

- At least 80 % of the occupied units include at least one resident age fifty-five or older and the community follows a policy that demonstrates intent to provide housing for those ages fifty-five or older.

HOPA also did away with a previous requirement that age-restricted housing provide "significant services and facilities specifically designed to meet the physical and social needs of older persons." Therefore, many stand-alone care facilities, such as assisted living and skilled nursing facilities, are not age-restricted even though they are sometimes referred to as "retirement homes." While the vast majority of residents are older in age, a growing number of young people are entering these care facilities following major accidents or illnesses that hinder their ability to live independently.

In this chapter I will categorize different types of retirement communities but I urge you not to get too caught up in specific labels. Instead, I recommend that you learn what to look for in terms of services provided, particularly as it relates to health care services, and consider how those services match up to your desires and objectives.

Aside from the more obvious characteristics, such as size of the community, amenities, culture and location, one of the most important factors to consider when distinguishing one retirement community from another is which phase(s) along the continuum of care the community places its focus.

The term "continuum of care" refers to the increasing intensity of health care services that may be required as a person ages; beginning with independent living and progressing to personal care or assisted living and then around-the-clock skilled care. Different retirement communities focus on different points along the continuum, while some retirement communities provide services spanning the entire continuum.

Here is a description of each of the main phases along the continuum:

Independent Living

Independent living represents the beginning phase of the continuum. It includes those who are mostly able to perform the normal activities of daily living without the assistance of another person and do not require on-going medical supervision. However, occasional assistance with daily chores and other tasks may be required. These everyday tasks are sometimes referred to as "Instrumental Activities of Daily Living" (IADLs).

Assisted Living

The definition of assisted living varies widely depending on the source. Sometimes referred to as "custodial care" or "personal care," assisted living is considered non-medical care and is designed for individuals who require assistance with one or more of the six Activities of Daily Living (ADLs)—eating, bathing, dressing, toileting, transferring (walking) and continence.

I want to reiterate an important point, which is that assisted living focuses only on non-medical care. While recipients of assisted living services are not able to live completely independently they do not require the level of medical care offered in a skilled nursing facility (SNF).

Assisted living services may be provided at home or in a facility. Quite often assisted living is received first in the home.

Yet, as a higher level of assistance is required some families may determine that moving to an Assisted Living Facility (ALF) is the most logical alternative. The range and level of assisted living services varies from one ALF to another. Around-the-clock care may be available in some ALFs, but not the type of professional medical care offered by a skilled nursing facility.

Skilled Care / Skilled Nursing Care (and Memory Care)

The Centers for Medicare and Medicaid Services (CMS) describe Skilled Care as "A type of health care given when you need skilled nursing or rehabilitation staff to manage, observe, and evaluate your care. Nursing, physical therapy, occupational therapy, and speech therapy are considered skilled care by Medicare. In addition to providing direct care these professionals manage, observe, and evaluate your care."[12] This type of care may be provided by a Licensed Nurse Practitioner or therapist but not necessarily by a Registered Nurse.

Skilled Nursing Care, on the other hand, is defined as "Care given or supervised by Registered Nurses. Nurses provide direct care; manage, observe, and evaluate a patient's care, and teach the patient and his or her family caregiver. Examples include: giving IV drugs, shots, or tube feedings; changing dressings; and teaching about diabetes care."[13]

Although Skilled Care and Skilled Nursing Care are often provided in a facility setting, there are also licensed home health care providers that deliver such care at home.

12 U.S. Centers for Medicare and Medicaid Services (CMS). *Medicare.gov.* Web. http://www.medicare.gov/homehealthcompare/Resources/Glossary.html

13 U.S. Centers for Medicare and Medicaid Services (CMS). *Medicare.gov.* Web. http://www.medicare.gov/homehealthcompare/Resources/Glossary.html

In addition to what I have described above, Memory Care is becoming a more common aspect of Assisted Living and Skilled Care. Mainly focused on those with Dementia and Alzheimer's disease, Memory Care is usually offered in a facility setting and the level of care increases as the severity of the illness progresses, often leading to full 24-hour care.

Now that you have a better understanding of the continuum of care, let's begin exploring the different types of retirement communities. The retirement communities covered in this chapter focus almost entirely on those who are either at the very beginning of the continuum of care (fully independent) or more towards the middle (limited assisted living needs).

Purpose-Built or Naturally Occurring

Most retirement communities are defined as "purpose-built." This means they were developed specifically with the purpose of being age-qualified. However, a small but growing number of retirement communities are being classified as "naturally occurring retirement communities (NORCs)," due to the fact that residents of a particular neighborhood aged together over time and/or have experienced a large number of older residents moving into the community.

NORCs are emerging as an attractive way for older Americans to remain in their homes for a longer period of time by providing services geared towards the specific needs of their residents and with the goal of increasing healthy aging behaviors. NORCs range in size and can be found in low income areas as well as more affluent areas. No matter the location or resident demographics, the key to a successful NORC is identifying the unique needs of the community and providing the appropriate services to meet those needs. Services may include social and health care services, individual risk assessments and follow-up, transportation, case management, educational and exercise programs, and more. These programs are often privately run but sometimes partner with local and state agencies. See the resources section in the back of this book to find out where you can learn more about NORCs.

Active Adult Communities

Active Adult Communities are generally "purpose-built" developments that cater specifically to those who are able to live independently but seek a low-maintenance lifestyle. A key feature that distinguishes Active Adult Communities from most other retirement communities is that residents own their homes or units. Many Active Adult Communities offer free standing homes but they may also include condominiums, townhomes, and multi-family housing units. Since most residents are still quite active, the communities are often developed in close proximity to desirable attractions such as shopping centers, theatres, performing arts centers, and parks.

While interior maintenance and household chores are still the responsibility of the homeowner, low maintenance or maintenance-free exteriors are usually offered and paid for by the resident through home owners' association (HOA) dues. This allows residents to enjoy other aspects of their retirement years without the added burden of maintaining the yard or attending to other chores related to exterior home maintenance. Aside from the HOA dues (and a mortgage payment if applicable) there are no other monthly service fees required.

Active Adult Communities do not offer a central dining facility or other common spaces often found in other types of retirement communities, although many will offer recreational spaces such as golf courses, tennis courts and clubhouses.

Essentially, Active Adult Communities are no different from other residential communities except for the age 55+ requirement and, in some cases, the fact that the floor plans may be designed more specifically for those of older ages. They do not provide assisted living or health care of any form, and do not have health care facilities on site. For this reason it could be said that those who live in Active Adult Communities still fall under the "aging at home" category.

If you or a loved one desires to live in a retirement community that is equipped to provide long-term care or nursing care services then an active adult community would not be the appropriate choice. Of course, arranging for in-home care is an option and some Active Adult Communities may have contracted arrangements with third-party home care service providers.

Independent Living Communities

Independent Living Communities are often referred to as rental retirement communities or supportive living communities and cater to those who seek to remain "comfortably independent," or mostly independent. Independent Living Communities are rental-based; therefore, they do not require the purchase of a unit or an entry fee. Independent Living Communities typically feature apartment style living as opposed to free standing homes, though this is not always the case.

According to the National Investment Center for the Seniors Housing and Care Industry (NIC), Independent Living Communities offer "...central dining facilities that provide residents, as part of their monthly fee, access to meals and other services such as housekeeping, linen service, transportation, and social and recreational activities."[14] Unlike Active Adult Communities, Independent Living Communities provide interior maintenance and other in-home services.

Upon first glance, an Independent Living Community might be confused with an Assisted Living Facility. The general concept behind Independent Living Communities is to help residents remain in their independent living units for as long as possible, thus delaying the need to move to an off-site care facility. Therefore "supportive services" are available for residents in their living units, although they are usually rather limited and more intermittent compared to what you might find in a stand-alone care facility. All such services are paid for by the resident at the full market rate and are not included in the monthly rental fee.

Supportive services offered in Independent Living Communities are generally not provided directly by staff of the community, except perhaps for household chores and interior maintenance. Instead, assisted living services are offered through outside providers with which the community has contracted. Although the community makes these services available, a resident usually is not required to use the same care provider with which the community has contracted.

---

14 National Investment Center (NIC) for the Seniors Housing and Care Industry and American Seniors Housing Association, *Classifications for Seniors Housing Property Types* (Annapolis, MD: NIC, 2014) http://www.nic.org/research/classifications.aspx

Independent Living Communities do not feature on-site health care facilities. If a resident should require a higher level of assisted living or skilled nursing care they would need to move to an off-site care facility. To help make such a transition easier some newer Independent Living Communities are being developed within close proximity to separately owned care facilities.

Senior Living Apartments

Senior Living Apartments could be considered a close cousin of Independent Living Communities. The two terms are often used interchangeably because both offer pure rental arrangements on an age-restricted basis but there are a few differences. Senior Living Apartments are often viewed as a more affordable alternative to Independent Living Communities, mainly because they provide fewer services.

According to the NIC's definition one of the key differences between Independent Living Communities and Senior Living Apartments is the absence of a central dining facility. They define Senior Apartments as "multifamily residential rental properties restricted to adults at least 55 years of age or older. These properties do not have central kitchen facilities and generally do not provide meals to residents, but may offer community rooms, social activities, and other amenities." Like Independent Living Communities, Senior Apartments do not have a health care facility on site and do not directly provide assisted living or health care, but may contract with outside providers for supportive services.

Some Senior Apartments are classified as "affordable senior housing," which qualify for HUD supported government subsidies to help provide affordable rent or rent based on income.

Cooperative Senior Housing

Although it makes up only a small portion of the retirement housing market today, an increasingly popular retirement housing choice for those who are able to live independently is known as Cooperative Housing. There are approximately 103 retirement housing Co-Ops in the United States and the vast majority of them are currently found in Minnesota, where favorable financing at the state level has allowed development to thrive more than in other states. Approximately fifteen Co-Ops are also located in neighboring Iowa.

On the surface, a Cooperating Housing Community may appear similar to an Active Adult Community or an Independent Living Community. Co-Ops offer maintenance free living and other services, but they are unique in the fact that the houses (including free standing homes, townhomes, or apartments) and the land are owned by a Cooperative Corporation. The stock of the corporation is owned by the residents, or "members."

According to the Senior Cooperative Foundation website, "cooperatively owned senior housing provides full apartment and townhouse living, controlled by the seniors themselves. All financial benefits accrue to the senior owners, including return of equity upon resale."[15] Many Co-Ops reflect the mentality of their members, as the sense of belonging and cooperation among residents is one of the key benefits of living in such a community.

15 Senior Cooperative Foundation. http://www.seniorcoops.org/

When someone buys into a Co-Op they are buying a share of the corporation, which provides exclusive rights to live in a particular unit. The share price typically represents a percentage of the unit's value, which is based on a number of factors, including location, services, and size of the unit. According to the Senior Cooperative Housing website this percentage is usually somewhere in the range of 35-50% of the purchase price. The remainder of the cost and other operating expenses are covered under the monthly service fee.

Pricing for Co-Ops is sometimes impacted by a practice called "limited appreciation," which seeks to limit the appreciation of the stock's value. Although it may seem counterintuitive, the purpose of this practice is to help ensure a timelier resale of the stock when a resident needs to move. The concept is that over time, units become more affordable and waiting lists build more easily. The cost of buying into a Co-Op that utilizes limited appreciation will likely be more affordable than purchasing a home or paying an entrance fee for a similarly sized unit in another community. One key reason why a timelier resale of a home is particularly helpful is because if a resident of a Co-Op moves out of the community, or at time of death, the monthly service fee must continue to be paid until the unit is resold.

The development of Co-Ops are often financed using "master mortgages" that are insured by the state through the Department of Housing and Urban Development (HUD). In this case, resident members pay monthly charges to cover their share of operating expenses for the community, as well as real estate taxes and debt service on their share of the master mortgage.

In effect, members of Co-Ops are their own landlords. Although resident members do not directly own real estate in a Co-Op, they are often still considered homeowners and may therefore be entitled to deduct on their personal income taxes their share of interest on the master mortgage (check with your tax accountant on this to be sure).

As with the previous types of retirement community described, Co-Ops do not have health care facilities on site and do not directly provide any level of long-term care of skilled nursing care. In-home care and services may be arranged with outside providers and the resident is responsible for the full cost of those services.

I will dedicate the next two chapters entirely to a hybrid type of retirement community, which is sometimes referred to as a "Full Service Retirement Community." This includes a broader array of services and choices; often in exchange for a higher financial commitment on the part of the resident.

CHAPTER 3

How is a Full Service Retirement Community Unique from Other Retirement Communities?

An increasingly popular, but often complex, retirement living alternative is the Continuing Care Retirement Community, or CCRC. Often referred to as "Full Service Retirement Communities," CCRCs provide a broad range of services usually spanning the full continuum of care. In general, CCRCs combine one or more of the previously mentioned types of communities with the availability of an on-site health care facility, often including assisted living and skilled nursing services.

A recent study of retirement perspectives conducted by Merrill Lynch in partnership with AgeWave revealed that three of the top four concerns among retirees associated with living a long life are 1) serious health problems, 2) not being a burden on family, and 3) becoming lonely.[16] For those who

---

16 Merrill Lynch and Age Wave. "Americans' Perspectives on New Retirement Realitities and the Longevity Bonus." Survey. Dec. 2012- Jan. 2013. http://wealthmanagement.ml.com/publish/content/application/pdf/GWMOL/2013_Merrill_Lynch_Retirement_Study.pdf

share these concerns, a Full Service Retirement Community may be a wonderful solution. Yet choosing the right community is a significant and often complex decision.

CCRCs are regulated at the state level; therefore, each state has its own definition of what constitutes a CCRC. Additionally there is no standard industry definition. The NIC defines CCRCs as "Age-restricted properties that include a combination of independent living, assisted living and skilled nursing services (or independent living and skilled nursing) available to residents all on one campus. Resident payment plans vary and include entrance fee, condo/co-op and rental programs."[17] Although the NIC's definition says health care services are "available," many CCRCs go a step further by contractually guaranteeing access to health care. Additionally, some definitions do not specifically state that the health care facility be located on the same campus with independent living.

The large majority, approximately 80%, of Full Service Retirement Communities are not-for-profit communities. This means that they are typically sponsored by or affiliated with faith-based organizations, health systems, fraternal organizations, universities, etc. In recent years more for-profit providers have entered the market due in large part to favorable financing arrangements. See Chapter 5 for more information on differences between for-profit and not-for-profit providers.

The general appeal of a Full Service Retirement Community is that a resident who is either fully or mostly independent today, has peace of mind knowing that they live in a

17 National Investment Center (NIC) for the Seniors Housing and Care Industry and American Seniors Housing Association, Classifications for Seniors Housing Property Types (Annapolis, MD: NIC, 2014) http://www.nic.org/research/classifications.aspx

community which is equipped to provide health care services that may be required in the future. This can help to lift part of the burden that might otherwise fall on the adult children or other family members. Those who choose to move to Full Service Requirement Communities are usually planners; they prefer to take a proactive approach in addressing their future housing and health care needs.

Ideally, moving to a CCRC should be the last residency decision a person ever has to make. This is beneficial because moving only gets tougher as one gets older. However, it is also a mental stumbling block for some who have trouble getting past the thought that they are making their final move in life.

Newsweek contributor, Philip Moeller touches on this in his article, *Aging Insights: Residents Share What It's Like to Live in a Retirement Community*, whereby he summarizes a series of interviews he conducted with several residents of a community in Maryland to gather their perspective about life at a CCRC. Moeller states, "No one thought of where they now live as a retirement home. With many people still active in their 80s and 90s, the residents stressed that a retirement community is a place to live, not a place to get ready to die."[18]

Whether or not one chooses to move to a CCRC, the lifestyle and health care challenges associated with aging must still be confronted eventually. The question is whether you want to live in a community that is already equipped to support your needs when that time comes, and if you are willing and able to pay for this assurance.

---

18 Moeller, Philip. "Aging Insights: Residents Share What It's Like to Live in a Retirement Community." *U.S. News and World Report.* U.S. News and World Report, 20 Aug. 2013. Web. 9 Sept. 2013.

http://money.usnews.com/money/blogs/the-best-life/2013/08/20/aging-insights-residents-share-what-its-like-to-live-in-a-retirement-community

In order to better understand how Full Service Retirement Communities differ from other retirement living choices here are descriptions of a few key characteristics:

Contractually Guarantee a Continuum of Care

In its truest form a Continuing Care Retirement Community contractually guarantees access to a full continuum of care; usually for a period of time greater than one year and sometimes for life. The contract between the community and the resident is typically referred to as a "Residency and Care Contract." Alternatively, some CCRCs provide access to health care services but do not contractually guarantee such services for any period of time.

Entry and Monthly Fees

A large majority of CCRCs require an entry fee, although a growing number of communities are starting to offer rental contracts. Entry fees range anywhere from under $50,000 and go all the way up to $1 million and beyond. The average entry fee for a CCRC is just over $240,000.[19]

The ways in which entry fees are set by a community depends on the type of residency contract and the associated business model. In some cases a portion of the entry fee goes towards pre-payment of future health care services. In many cases a portion of the entry fee is set aside for long-term maintenance costs. There can be a wide variety of ways that entry fees may be used by the community.

---

19 National Investment Center (NIC), *NIC Investment Guide- Investing in Seniors Housing & Care Properties*. 2nd Edition. p.,91(Annapolis, MD: NIC, 2012).

If any portion of the entry fee is determined to be pre-payment of future health care costs, then part of the fee may be deductible by the resident as a health care expense. In some cases this deduction can be quite significant. If you are considering an entry fee CCRC you should consult with your tax advisor as well as a representative of the community to determine if a deduction is available.

Virtually all CCRCs require residents to pay a monthly service fee, even if an entry fee has been paid. Yet, for those communities that require an entry fee, the monthly service fee will likely be lower than what might be found at a comparable rental community.

Health Requirements

Prospective residents of CCRCs must be able to live independently in order to enter into a continuing care contract. They may be asked to fill out a health questionnaire or submit to a medical exam. Sometimes a representative of the community will request to order medical records on the prospective resident. (Some CCRCs allow direct entry into the health care facility but these residents do not participate in a continuing care contract.)

Although it is more applicable to some CCRCs than others, depending on the type of residency contract offered, the general reason for the health care screening is that CCRCs operate like insurance companies in the sense that the independent residents help offset some portion of the cost for those that require care.

Mark Miles of Crown Research Corporation addresses this matter in his article, *Evolution of the Old Folks Home* by stating, "The operators of traditional CCRCs find themselves in the self-insurance business and are forced to spread substantial risk over a relatively small population of residents."[20]

In his article, *Practice Development Opportunities for CPAs Assisting Older Clients with Housing Decisions*, Jim Sullivan also touches on this by saying, "If a higher than expected number of residents requires care, the facility may run into financial difficulty."[21]

Financial Requirements

In addition to health requirements, new residents of CCRCs often must pass financial requirements. Since the retirement community is committing to providing healthcare services to the resident, they want as much assurance as possible that the resident will be in a position financially to pay the ongoing monthly services fees and any fees that might be associated with health care services.

Of course, on the other side of the coin, if the community is too strict, it runs the risk of narrowing the pool of prospective residents too much and thus having units sit empty, which amounts to lost revenue.

---

20 Miles, Mark. "Evolution of the Old Folks Home." *Crown Research*. Crown Research Corporation. 25 July 2005. Web. 14 Aug. 2013. http://www. crownresearch.com/OJA.htm

21 Sullivan, Jim. "Practice Development Opportunities for CPAs Assisting Older Clients with Housing Decisions." *American Institute of CPAs.* American Institute of CPAs. 9 Aug. 2010. Web. 2 Oct. 2013. http://www. aicpa.org/Publications/Newsletters/AICPACPAInsider/2010/aug9/Pages/ PracticeDevelopmentOpportunity.aspx

A Focus on Wellness and Active Lifestyles

Virtually all retirement communities have a financial incentive to keep residents healthy. A recent article released by the Assisted Living Federation of America states, "Senior living communities are discovering the many benefits of fitness programs. Effective wellness programs can decrease falls, reduce agitation in seniors with Alzheimer's, and significantly decrease the costs for senior living providers."[22] Because of their unique business model, CCRCs have even more incentive to help keep residents healthy and independent.

Comprehensive health and wellness programs at CCRCs may include access to qualified fitness professionals, special-diet meal plans, aquatic and fitness centers, low-impact aerobics and yoga classes. Wellness programs are not always limited to the physical aspects. More CCRCs today are emphasizing the "whole person" concept, including emotional, spiritual, intellectual, vocational and social experiences.

According to *Today's Continuing Care Retirement Community*, "An overall objective of any CCRC is to create an environment and choices that enable older adults to experience fully actualized, creative and satisfying aging."[23] This often includes having a number of common areas onsite to accommodate socialization and activities, as well as other amenities such as auditoriums and theatres, ballrooms for parties and celebrations, woodworking shops, and business

22 "Reaping the Financial Benefits of Investing in Wellness Programs." *Assisted Living Federation of America (ALFA)*. Assisted Living Federation of America. 8 Jan. 2014. http://www.alfa.org/News/2547/Reaping-the-Financial-Benefits-of-Investing-in-Wellness-Programs

23 LeadingAge and American Seniors Housing Association (ASHA). *Today's Continuing Care Retirement Community (CCRC)*. (Washington, DC: LeadingAge, and Washington, DC: ASHA, 2010).

centers. On-site lifelong learning programs and easy access to the broader community through service programs are also becoming increasingly common.

CHAPTER 4

How Do I Interpret the Various Residency Contracts Offered by Full Service Retirement Communities?

When considering a Continuing Care Retirement Community it is important to understand the type of contract that is offered and how it might impact the total cost over your lifetime. In some cases a single community may offer several different contracts from which to choose.

Most contracts offered by CCRCs fall under one of five major types as described in the chart below:

Entry-fee contracts

Type A "Full Life Care"	Type B "Modified"	Type C "Fee for Service"	Rental "Fee for Service"	Equity/Co-Op
• Pre-pay for unlimited care • Monthly fee does not increase for cost of care • Predictable expenses for resident • CCRC absorbs more risk for the cost of care	• Pre-pay for some amount of care • Certain # of free days in health care center, or a discount off market rate • CCRC and resident share cost of care risk	• No pre-pay for care • Cost of care will be full market rate • Services may be bundled or unbundled • Resident absorbs cost of care risk • Monthly expenses less predictable	• No entry fee - maybe a nominal "Community Fee" • Higher monthly fees • Access to care generally not guaranteed • Possibly fewer services and amenities	• Resident purchases home or shares in a corporation • Monthly service fees still apply • Cost of care typically at market rate, i.e. "fee for service"

In theory, each type of contract should be actuarially equivalent. In other words, if you use the same assumptions and work off of averages, the numbers should come out about the same in the end regardless of the contract chosen. Yet, different communities may use different methods to "price" their contracts so this theory will not always hold true when comparing one community to another.

The first three contract types shown in the chart above involve entry fees. Among the entry fee contracts there is a tradeoff between the amount of the entry fee and the cost of healthcare services. The contract with the highest entry fee is not necessarily the one that will cost the most over lifetime.

For instance, all other things being equal, (i.e. location, size of unit, amenities, etc.) a resident will pay a higher entry fee for a Type-A (life-care) contract than for a Type-C (fee-for-service) contract. But here is the tradeoff: Although the resident pays more up-front, their monthly fees will not increase should they ever need to move into the health care center, regardless of how long they are in the facility. This does not mean the monthly service fees will never increase. There may be occasional increases to reflect the impact of inflation on operating costs or other ancillary expenses, such as prescription management services. Yet the resident will not pay additional amounts directly related to the cost of primary health care services provided. The biggest advantage of a life-care contract is that the resident has capped most of their out-of-pocket housing and long-term care expenses for life, with the exception of ancillary expenses that may arise. The risk, however, is that the resident is paying more up-front for care that may or may not be required in the future.

A resident with a Type-C contract, by contrast, will pay a lower entry fee, but if assisted living or skilled nursing care is required, then the monthly service fee will increase to the full market rate of such care. This could potentially amount to a monthly increase of thousands of dollars per month. The risk of a Type-C contract is that residents are exposed to unlimited risk in terms of the amount of healthcare services they may require and the corresponding costs. Some of this risk could be mitigated by owning long-term care insurance. (For information on the relationship between long-term care insurance and CCRC contracts see Chapter 6.)

Type-B contracts are essentially a balance between Type-A and Type-C, whereby the entry fee will cover the cost for some amount of future health care, but not an unlimited amount. This discount may be 30-40% for the cost of care in some cases. In other cases, monthly fees will still increase to reflect the full cost of care but the contract allows for a certain number of free days in the health care center before the increase begins. These free days may be offered on a per-year basis, or over the life of the contract.

For people who like the idea of access to a continuum of care but do not want to pay an entry fee, a Rental Contract might make sense. All other things being equal, the monthly service fee for a Rental Contract will likely be higher than other contract types since no money is paid up-front in the form of an entry fee. Additionally, while access to health care is available, it may not be contractually guaranteed, as is often the case with the other contract types described above. Like Type-C contracts, residents with Rental Contracts will pay full market rate for care provided in the health care center.

Finally, some CCRCs operate as Equity Communities or Co-Ops. Residents in Equity Communities actually own their home or unit but are still required to pay a monthly service fee to the community. Residents of Co-Op CCRCs have purchased shares of the corporation and also pay a monthly service fee. Under both arrangements, health care services will usually be offered at the full market rate or at a slight discount.

Refundable Entry fee Contracts

Entry fees are almost always refundable, up to a certain point, if the resident moves out or at death; in which case the refund would go to the resident's heirs or the estate. Standard contracts offered by CCRCs are usually "declining balance" contracts. Under a standard, declining-balance contract the entry fee will be completely earned or amortized by the CCRC over the first few years, after which time the resident will not receive back any portion of their entrance fee. Prior to end of this period of time, however, some portion of the entrance fee would be returned, according to where they fall on the amortization schedule at that point.

Here is an example of how a standard amortization contract works:

The standard contract entry fee for a two bedroom cottage at ABC Community is $260,000. Under the standard contract the community earns 4% up-front and then it earns 2% each month for the next four years; a total of 100%. If the resident moves out of the CCRC or passes away in the thirty-sixth month, for instance, then 76% of the entry fee stays

with the community [4% + (2% times 36 months)].
The remaining 24% would go to the resident, or
the resident's heirs. If the resident is still living in
the community after four years, there would be no
remaining refund available from that point forward.

In addition to, or in place of, the declining balance
contract, some CCRCs offer a different type of refundable
contract. This is often referred to as a "return of capital" plan,
in which some portion of the entry fee is refundable regardless
of how long the resident residents in the community. Common
refundable contracts are 50%, 75%, 90% and even 100%.

Here is an example of how a return of capital plan works:

ABC Community also offers a 50% refund option. If
the resident elects this option, the entry fee for the
exact same unit used in the example above is now
$360,000; an increase of 38% over the standard
contract fee. In this case, the community immediately
earns 4% of the entrance fee up-front and then earns
2% per month for the next twenty-three months; a
total of 50% earned by the community. After two
years the community does not earn any more of the
entrance fee. In this example, the resident, or the
resident's estate, is guaranteed to receive back a
minimum of $180,000 [50% x $360,000] no matter
how long they live in the community, and possibly
more if the occurrence takes place within the first two
years.

Those who choose a return-of-capital contract should be
clear about the stipulations for receiving the refund. For instance, does the unit have to be re-occupied before the refund

will be paid? If so, is the monthly fee required to be paid until such time as the unit is re-occupied? Is there a maximum time limit whereby you will receive the refund regardless of whether the unit is re-occupied or not? Requiring the monthly fee to continue until re-occupancy is a double-edged sword. This provision helps provide financial stability for the community because it essentially means that there are no vacant units on site, but it is not always viewed favorably by the resident or the resident's heirs who have to bear the burden of the payments until re-occupancy.

CCRC Without Walls

In addition to the contract types described above, there is a relatively new and innovative type of contract being offered by some Full Service Retirement Communities, which is called "CCRC Without Walls." This contract provides access to the same continuum of care and many of the other services offered by the CCRC but instead of moving into the community, the member remains in their own home until such time as they are ready to move into the community. This approach will likely play a big role in the future of CCRCs as they seek to attract more seniors who want to stay at home as long as possible but like the concept of guaranteed access to care at a predictable price.

A CCRC Without Walls contract is not the same as simply purchasing services on an as-needed basis. According to Stephen Maag of LeadingAge, "The important difference is a CCRC without walls program takes the concept of a Life Care contract [Type-A] and a bundle of services into the home. A CCRC Without Walls contract is a comprehensive approach to providing the health and wellness lifestyle to seniors in their homes. It is not just services which can be purchased on an as needed basis."[24]

Depending on the selected plan, a one-time enrollment fee and monthly fee is required, and a bundle of services is available to the member in their own home. If and when the member wishes to move to the CCRC they will have priority over non-members and the cost for health care services will remain the same as the monthly fee the member was paying while living at home. Entry fees and monthly service fees are much lower than what would be required if moving into the community.

---

24 Maag, Stephen. *CCRC Without Walls: Care Models of the Future.* (Washington, DC: LeadingAge, 2012).

CHAPTER 5

What Else Should I Know about Full Service Retirement Communities?

When someone chooses to move to a Full Service Retirement Community, they are placing their trust in the community to provide housing and health care for the rest of their life. Likewise, the community is making a significant commitment to the resident to provide such housing and care. While CCRCs want some level of assurance that a new resident's finances are adequate to cover the costs associated with living in the community, the resident should also take time to check out the finances of the community to be sure it can uphold its commitment. Prospective residents should also check out the quality of health care provided. After all, access to health care is one of the main reasons for choosing a Full Service Retirement Community.

Financial Viability

Very few CCRCs have actually experienced bankruptcy. As described in the document *CCRCs Today*, prepared by LeadingAge, since the time of the great recession in 2008 the percentage of bankruptcies among CCRCs through January of 2011 has been approximately 1 %. The report goes on to state, "Several [bankruptcies] were related directly or indirectly to new developments, others were CCRCs in markets where housing prices crashed and seniors were unable to sell their homes. While these bankruptcies are difficult for all involved, in ALL cases the CCRC remained open and the residents were not forced to relocate."[25] Since 2011 there have only been a handful of CCRC bankruptcies nationwide so the overall percentage of bankruptcies has continued to remain very low.

As indicated above, many of the communities that have experienced financial strain are newer developments. In his article *Lessons from CCRC Bankruptcies: Put Skin in the Game*, Robert Carr, contributing writer for National Real Estate Investor, states, "The bankruptcies that beset a number of seniors housing properties in the past seven years can be traced back to mostly timing issues, opening up at or near the height of the recession..."[26]

Nonetheless, the entire CCRC industry, as with most other industries, was impacted by the economic downturn of 2008. One of the main reasons is that prospective residents of Full Service Retirement Communities often rely on the ability to sell their home and use the equity to pay the entry fee. As a result of the recession and the deeply depressed housing market it became more difficult for people to sell their

25 Maag, Stephen. *CCRCs Today.* (Washington, DC: LeadingAge, 2012). http://www.leadingage.org/uploadedFiles/Content/Members/CCRCs/Marketing/CCRCs_Today_01_17_12.pdf

26 Carr, Robert. "Lesson From CCRC Bankruptcies: Put Skin in the Game." *National Real Estate Investor.* 28 Jan. 2013. Web. 10 Oct. 2014. http://nreionline.com/seniors-housing/lesson-ccrc-bankruptcies-put-skin-game

homes. Therefore, the CCRC industry experienced declining occupancy numbers. CCRCs who had waiting lists in the past now found themselves struggling to fill new units. Although the number of actual bankruptcies has been minimal some communities have had to cut services or raise fees, or both.

In 2009, the U.S. Senate Special Committee on Aging released a report highlighting the potential risks. Here is an excerpt from the report:

> "The CCRC model is particularly vulnerable during economic downturns, as stagnant real estate markets drive down occupancy levels in independent living units, which serve as CCRCs' primary source of profit."[27]

The report goes on to state:

> "Evaluating the merits and judging the financial health of a CCRC is extremely challenging for an individual consumer without professional assistance."

Overall, the industry has weathered the storm well. Although difficulties continue, the industry has learned from the experience and market conditions are improving. In late 2013 Fitch Ratings revised its outlook on the not-for-profit CCRC industry (which makes up about 80% of the industry) from negative to stable, citing positive housing market signs, improvement in access to capital, stabilized occupancy rates, and stable financial performance.[28] The Fitch report describes

---

27 United States. Senate Special Committee on Aging. *Continuing Care Retirement Communities: Risks to Seniors- Summary of Committee Investigation, Majority Staff.* Washington, DC. 21 July 2010. Web. 7 Aug. 2013.

28 Fitch Ratings, *2014 Outlook Stable for U.S. Nonprofit CCRCs (New York, NY: Fitch Ratings 2013).*

how the not-for-profit CCRC sector remains susceptible to external forces such as a slow-moving economy, global financial issues, and housing market recovery but also that the industry has adapted strategies to address these matters and how the sector has largely begun to see positive momentum in performance.

There are a number of factors that could ultimately impact the financial stability of a CCRC, many of which are beyond the scope of this book, but I want to provide a few helpful guidelines to help get you started.

There are both qualitative and quantitative aspects that apply when researching the financial stability of a CCRC. It is important not to put too much weight in any one of the following items because very few communities will excel in every single area.

Instead, you should consider the strength of these components as a whole. Be sure to see the resources section in the back to find out where you can learn more.

Qualitative

- Management and Board of Directors: Is the management team and board of directors experienced in a variety of business backgrounds, including health care and long-term care, real estate finance, hospitality management, insurance, accounting, and more?

- Established or Start-Up: Many CCRC bond defaults occur when start-up communities fall short on achieving the desired level of occupancy in the expected time frame. This does not mean you should avoid start-up communities altogether but you should take extra time to learn about the financing of the community and if they are on track to meeting their short-term occupancy goals. Also ask if the developer has put up their own equity or if they have borrowed the majority of the funds for development.

- Rated Debt: Although this only applies to a small percentage of CCRCs, some organizations that finance development or expansion using debt may choose have the debt rated by one of the major rating agencies such as Standard & Poors or Fitch. The debt rating is a strong indicator of a community's financial stability. Very few CCRCs have ratings higher than BBB.

- Waiting List: Although far more common prior to the recession than today waiting lists tend to indicate strong demand, particularly if getting on the waiting list requires a non-refundable fee.

- Accreditation: Is the community accredited by the Continuing Care Accreditation Commission (CCAC)? The CCAC is a division of the Commission on Accreditation of Rehabilitation (CARF) and is currently the only national accrediting body for continuing care retirement communities. The significance of accreditation is widely debated among representatives of the CCRC industry but part of the accreditation process is an analysis of financial and operating standards. Keep in mind that accreditation is voluntary and costly. Just because a CCRC is not accredited does not mean it is not financially sound.

- Type of Resident Contract(s): Type-A and Type-B contracts carry more financial risk for the retirement community. Again, I am not suggesting you exclude from your search communities offering these contracts. Yet, sound finances are particularly important for these communities because of the long-term financial commitment they are making to their residents.

Quantitative

- Financial Ratios: You may wish to have a qualified financial professional help you to analyze a community's financial ratios which encompass liquidity, debt, and operating margins. (If a CCRC is part of a multi-site parent organization then the finances of the overall operation are important to consider in addition to those of the community itself.) Examples of ratios include days cash on hand, cash to debt, and net operating margins, to name a few.

- Occupancy Level: Maintaining a high level of stabilized occupancy is important for CCRCs because empty units are a cost drain. Rating agencies have traditionally looked for occupancy levels above 90% across all levels of care, although fewer communities surpass this level today than before the recession.

- Actuarial Analysis: Does the community regularly prepare an actuarial analysis to project the cost of providing future health care services to current residents? If so, is there a gap between the projected cost and the current funds set aside to pay for that care? Such a gap is referred to as a "Future Service Obligation (FSO)" and it indicates a short-fall in funding set aside for future obligations. This, too, is particularly important for Type-A and Type-B contracts.

- Ratio of Independent to Health care Residents: If a disproportionately high number of residents are receiving health care services, it will likely impact the overall finances of the community. Generally speaking, the percentage of the resident population receiving health care services should be less than about 20%.

I want to reiterate that there are additional factors that can impact financial stability other than what I have described above, but if a CCRC receives good marks in most of these areas and representatives of the community are willing and able to address these questions, then it is reasonable to assume that the CCRC is taking many of the necessary steps to maintain a strong financial outlook.

State Level Regulation

As I mentioned previously CCRCs are regulated at the state level. As of the writing of this book there are thirty-eight states that regulate CCRCs through various state divisions such as the Department of Insurance, Financial Services, Aging or Elder Services. The remaining twelve states and the District of Columbia currently have no regulatory structure in place. There are two states—Alaska and Wyoming—that do not have any CCRCs.

Regulation of Continuing Care Retirement Communities focuses mostly on the financial standing of a community. It applies to the entire operation, including independent living, and should not be confused with health care-related regulations. On-site health care facilities within a CCRC will be regulated separately by the appropriate licensing body of the state. Additionally, health care facilities that wish to receive Medicare and/or Medicaid reimbursements must be certified in accordance with federal and state guidelines for those programs. But these agencies do not regulate the operations and financial management of the entire community.

For those states which regulate CCRCs, the degree of oversight can vary drastically from one state to another, with some providing only minimal oversight. If the community you are considering is located in a state that regulates CCRCs, consider reaching out to the appropriate regulatory agency and ask about the financial requirements and oversight process for CCRCs, as well as any record of bankruptcy of CCRCs located within the state. Remember, however, that just because a CCRC is located in a state that is not regulated does not mean that it is not well-managed or financially viable.

Health Care

Although CCRCs offer many attractive services and amenities for those living independently, it's important to remember that one of the primary reasons for considering this type of retirement community is access to health care. Are representatives of the community open to discussing the health care services? Are they proud of their health care services or do they tend to avoid talking about the subject? What distinguishes their health care services from the competition?

When evaluating health care services in a CCRC, here are a few more things to consider:

- CMS Rating: If the community is Medicare-certified (as opposed to private pay only), then be sure to check out the CMS rating for the on-site health care facility at Medicare.gov under the section called "nursing home compare." As with accreditation, there are some in the industry that debate the methodology and accuracy of these ratings but this is just one more component to consider along with others. The Medicare website also provides an explanation of any marks against the care facility.

- Record of complaints: You may be able to find a list of complaints at Long-Term Care Ombudsman program for the state in which the retirement community is located.

- Observe: Some people prefer not to see the health care facility until they need care, but I encourage prospective residents to visit the health care center. Look to see if the nursing staff seems happy and productive. Does the facility appear well-kept and free of lingering odors?

- Staff turnover: Ask about the level of staff turnover in the health care facility. A high turnover rate might indicate an unhappy staff, which could translate into poor management and care. The industry average hovers around 30%.

- Ask Others: If you know someone who has a loved one that has received care in the facility ask about their experience.

For-Profit or Not- For-Profit

When I speak to various groups about CCRCs one of the things I hear people say most often is that not-for-profit CCRCs "won't kick you out if you run out of money." I want to briefly touch on this topic because, although it is not necessarily tied to a specific type of contract, the agreement between a resident and the community as spelled out in the Residency and Care Contract may be influenced by the tax status of the community.

In general it is true that not-for-profit providers will not force a resident to leave the community if their savings are depleted through no fault of their own. But this does not mean you should automatically exclude for-profit CCRCs from your search. The reality is that there are pros and cons to both. For-profit and not-for-profit CCRCs have a responsibility to act in the best interest of the overall community and, therefore, ultimately reserve the right to terminate the contract under certain circumstances, including lack of payment by the resident. Having said this, many not-for-profit communities have a proud track record of having never forced a resident to leave their community due to lack of funds.

Not-for-profits are mission driven. In fact, having a charitable mission of some form is required to maintain not-for-profit status. Oftentimes part of that mission is providing lifetime housing and health care services for residents; even if a resident's personal finances are depleted. Yet, at the end of the day, this all hinges on the community's ability to provide such support.

For example, contract language for a not-for-profit CCRC often reads something like this:

"The community may offer financial assistance to a resident who has encountered financial difficulty provided the resident has managed his or her personal resources properly after taking occupancy... such assistance will be conditional on the community's ability to provide funds while operating on a sound financial basis."

In the case of return-of-capital contracts financial as-sistance will typically come first out of any applicable refund before tapping into other resources. It is not uncommon for not-for-profit CCRCs to maintain a benevolent fund or "financial assistance fund" to help support residents in financial need. However, simply having such a fund does not necessarily guarantee financial assistance. The account needs to be adequately funded on an ongoing basis.

By contrast, for-profit CCRCs are generally less mission-driven and more profit-driven but this is not inherently bad. I think Ralph and Lori Smith best summarize the contrast in their book, "Worry-Free Retirement Living: Choosing a Full Service Retirement Community",[29] describing that not-for-profit CCRCs tend to make decisions with their hearts, which sometimes come at the expense of sound business judgment. For-profits, on the other hand, tend make decisions with their heads, which often leads to more sound business judgment, but perhaps at the expense of compassion. Ultimately both are important because all the compassion in the world does no good if the community does not remain financially viable.

For-profit CCRCs generally understand that it is good business practice to take care of their residents to the extent possible and do not want a reputation in the community of being uncompassionate. Sometimes a for-profit CCRC will even maintain separate charitable funds to provide financial aid for residents. However, the resident's estate may be responsible for repaying any deferred payments if possible.

As with any other aspect of the CCRC decision process this is a matter that you should discuss with a representative of the CCRC that you are considering, regardless of whether it is a not-for-profit or for-profit community. Ask about the community's specific policy and history of providing such any such

29 Smith, Ralph and Loni. *Worry-Free Retirement Living: Choosing a Full Service Retirement Community.* Baltimore: Publish America, 2005. Print

financial assistance, as well as the status and maintenance of any charitable or financial assistance funds.

CHAPTER 6

How Does Long-Term Care Impact My Retirement Housing Choice?

Choosing the retirement housing choice that is best for you depends a great deal on how you plan to address long-term care needs that you may encounter in the future. One choice is to age at home. Alternatively you could choose to move to a retirement community like one of those described in this book. One of the most obvious questions is whether you prefer to live someplace that's equipped to provide the care you may need in the future. Are you willing to potentially pay for the peace of mind that comes with that? In trying to answer these questions people often want to know the odds of requiring long-term care, the cost of care, and the resources available to help pay for care.

Before moving on I want to be clear about what I am referring to when I use the phrase "long-term care." For the purposes of this book "long-term care" includes assisted living services as well as skilled nursing care. As I will discuss shortly, there are some who question whether the definition of long-term care should include assisted living.

Also, be sure not to confuse the phrase "long-term care" with "long-term care insurance." I will refer to both in this chapter.

As it pertains to the odds of needing long-term care, there is a statement on the website for the American Association for Long-Term Care Insurance (AALTCI) that says the real risk of needing long-term care is either 0% (you will never need it) or 100% (you will need it). Obviously this is an overly simplified way of looking at the issue, but the point is that basing your planning on averages is not relevant to your own personal risk or situation. In other words, your experience ultimately may fall well outside of the averages so you need to plan for a broad range of possible scenarios.

One of the most frequently cited statistics is the one I referenced earlier from the Department of Health and Human Services (DHHS), which says that approximately 70% of people over age 65 will require some degree of long-term care services during their lifetime.[30] Some argue that this statistic is misleading because it includes not only those who require assistance with ADLs, as described in Chapter 2, but also those who require assistance with IADLs, such as homemaker services. For example, if someone over age 65 has a house-keeper come by once a week, is that considered long-term care? Most would say no, but conceivably the DHHS statistic includes this form of assistance. A separate statistic produced by AARP suggests that the lifetime probability of becoming disabled in at least two activities of daily living or of being

---

30 Long-TermCare.gov. *Who Needs Care?* United States Department of Health and Human Services. Web. 7 Jan. 2013. http://longtermcare.gov/the-basics/who-needs-care/

cognitively impaired, is 68 % for people age 65 and older.[31] However, neither of these statistics addresses the other part of the issue: how long care is needed.

According to the DHHS the average person over age 65 will require some level of long-term care (assistance with IADLs and/or ADLs) for approximately 3 years. When you look at women and men separately, a woman requires care for 3.7 years on average while men require care for 2.2 years on average. This means that the average traditional couple will require a combined 6 years of long-term care.

In terms of where care is provided, on average a person receives some degree of care at home for 2 years. This includes paid and unpaid care provided by a family member or friend, or a combination of both. The average stay in a health care facility, typically involving advanced assisted living services or skilled nursing care, is 1 year.[32]

Additionally, a statistic provided on the AALTCI website shows that for all long-term care insurance claims of at least 1 year or more, the average length of claim is 3.9 years.[33]

I want to reiterate that although it is helpful to understand these statistics, your personal experience or that of a loved one could fall well outside of the averages. You may know

31 American Association of Retired Persons (AARP). *Beyond 50.2003: A Report to the Nation on Independent Living and Disability, 2003,* (Washington: AARP 1 Jan 2005).

32 Long-TermCare.gov. *How Much Care Will You Need?* United States Department of Health and Human Services. Web. 7 Jan. 2013. http:// longtermcare.gov/the-basics/how-much-care-will-you-need/

33 American Association of Long-Term Care Insurance (AALTCI). *Long-Term Care Insurance Facts- Statistics.* Web. 3 Feb. 2014.

http://www.aaltci.org/long-term-care-insurance/learning-center/fast-facts.php

someone in your own life who has required care for a much longer period of time than the average.

What Does Long-Term Care Cost?

According to the most recent Genworth Cost of Care Study the average national cost for Home Care Provider is $18 per hour. [34] For a Home Health Aide the average is $19 per hour.

The national average cost for care in a one-bedroom, single occupancy unit at an Assisted Living Facility is $3,450 per month or $41,400 annually.

The national average daily rate for a private room in a Skilled Nursing Facility is $230. The average for a semi-private room is $207 per day. On an annual basis this comes to approximately $83,950 and $75,555 respectively.

Keep in mind that the figures I am providing here reflect national averages. The average cost per state or region will vary. The Genworth study is referenced in the resources section of this book and provides state-by-state averages.

Paying for Long-Term Care Services

The average person is often confused or misinformed about the various options that are available (or not available) to help pay for long-term care services and the amount of support available from each. The sources of payment for long-term care services can be broken down into two main categories: public (government-funded) programs and private pay. Public programs primarily include Medicare, Medicaid, and the

---

34 Genworth Financial, Inc. *Executive Summary- Genworth 2013 Cost of Care Survey,* (Richmond, VA: Genworth March 2013). https://www.genworth.com/dam/Americas/US/PDFs/Consumer/corporate/131168_031813_Executive%20Summary.pdf

Department of Veterans Affairs. Private pay options primarily include paying out-of-pocket and long-term care insurance.

Public Programs

Medicare

Medicare is a federal health insurance program that mostly provides health care coverage for those ages sixty-five and older. According to a recent report prepared by the Associated Press and the NORC Center for Public Affairs Research about half of all people age forty and older acknowledge that almost everyone will require some level of long-term care services in their life, even if they do not become seriously ill. The same report states that 44% believe Medicare will pay for ongoing long-term care services at home provided by a licensed home health care aid. And close to 40% believe Medicare will pay for ongoing services received in a nursing home.[35] The last two statistics reveal a major misconception among the public; that Medicare will cover long-term care and skilled care services indefinitely.

Medicare Part A and Part B are often referred to as traditional Medicare. Part A is generally considered to be hospital coverage and Part B is generally considered to be outpatient, physician coverage. Medicare supplement plans, often referred to as "Med-Sup Plans" and available through private insurance companies, cover gaps that Parts A and B may not

---

35 T. Tompson, J. Benz, D. Agiesta, K. Junius, and K. Lowell. *Long-Term Care: Perceptions, Experiences, and Attitudes Among Americans 40 and Older* (New York, NY: Associated Press 2013 and Chicago, IL: NORC at the University of Chicago 2013).

http://www.apnorc.org/PDFs/Long%20Term%20Care/AP_NORC_Long%20 Term%20Care%20Perception_FINAL%20REPORT.pdf include, such as coinsurance, co-pays, and deductibles. The key point to understand about Medicare is that it covers only *medically-necessary* care.

When it comes to long-term care services it gets a little tricky. Medicare Part A will cover medically necessary skilled nursing care, but only for a limited time and in a limited amount. The objective of Medicare is to get patients well as soon as possible and, therefore; the term you will most often hear as it pertains to Medicare's coverage of skilled nursing care is "rehab." Most often Medicare's coverage of skilled nursing care follows a serious medical occurrence, such as a stroke, heart attack, or major surgery. Medicare DOES NOT cover *non-medical*, assisted living care if that is the only type of care that is needed.

The full cost of skilled nursing care is covered by Medicare for the first 20 days. Between 21 and 100 days Medicare will pay up to $152 per day (in 2014). If skilled nursing care should be required for more than 100 days then Medicare ceases to provide coverage and the recipient of services is then required to pay 100% of the cost out-of-pocket. However, the 100 day period can reset in certain situations if there has been a substantial period of time between occurrences.

There are certain stipulations to that must be met before Medicare will pay. The recipient of care must have first had a hospital stay of at least 3 days or longer and admittance into the skilled nursing facility must take place within thirty days of the hospital stay. Additionally, care must be provided in a Medicare-certified facility. Medically necessary services provided at home by a Medicare-certified home health care agency may also qualify for Medicare coverage.

Medicaid

Unlike Medicare, which is a federal program, Medicaid is administered at the state level, although it does receive federal funding. The key difference is that Medicaid is designed specifically for low income households to help pay for medical expenses.

Also unlike Medicare, the Medicaid program will cover both skilled nursing care and assisted living services indefinitely. This usually occurs in a facility setting, although assistance does apply to at-home care in many instances.

Eligibility requirements vary by state but suffice it to say that, with the exception of a few allowances, in order to qualify for Medicaid you must have exhausted most of your financial resources and your income must be below an amount that is close to the federal poverty level. (Most states allow the cost of care to be deducted against income to determine if income eligibility requirements are met.) Medicaid will only be applicable if your provider, either the facility or a Home Care Provider, is Medicaid-certified.

Since Medicaid is designed to help those who are most in need financially, the government discourages people from giving away assets in order to qualify. A detailed summary is beyond the scope of this book but you should know that if you apply for Medicaid there will look at a 5-year look back period that begins immediately preceding the application whereby representatives of Medicaid will do an analysis to determine if any assets were given away during that period of time. If so then you will face a transfer penalty, which essentially means that before Medicaid kicks in you will first be required to pay for your own care up to an amount that is approximately equal the amount you gave away.

Department of Veterans Affairs

Veterans and surviving spouses of veterans are sometimes unaware of a valuable benefit available through the Office of Veterans Affairs' Administrations Aid and Attendance Program that helps cover the cost of assisted living at home or in a facility.

Qualification is not dependent on service-related injuries and can provide as much as $25,000 or more in annual benefit, depending on income levels and whether the recipient is married, single, or a surviving spouse of a veteran. A detailed analysis of qualifications can be found by referencing the resources listed in the back of this book but eligibility generally requires that the veteran must have received a discharge from service under any condition other than dishonorable and served at least 90 days of active military service, one day of which was during a war-time period. The applicant also must be a patient in a skilled nursing facility, be legally blind, confined to a bed, or have a documented need for assisted living services.

Private Pay

The term "private pay" simply means paying for necessary assisted living services or skilled nursing care using your own resources, without the assistance of government programs. Generally this means either paying for care out-of-pocket or using a personal insurance policy to cover some or all of the cost of care. If you find that a care facility describes itself as private pay it means that the facility does not accept Medicare or Medicaid reimbursements, although some facilities will accept one of these programs and not the other.

Long-term Care Insurance (LTCi)

Long-term care insurance is generally most appropriate for those who maintain a financial standing well above the level at which they would qualify for Medicaid, but not high enough to cover out-of-pocket the cost of care over an extended period of time. It's also appropriate for those who may desire to leave money to loved ones or charity instead of spending it on care.

In the early days of long-term care insurance most policies were considered pure nursing home policies. But many LTCi policies issued today cover care in assisted living and skilled care facilities, as well as in-home care and even adult day care. LTCi policies have certain "triggers" that determine what is required in order for a claim to be paid. The main trigger for the majority of policies will require that the policyholder be unable to perform at least 2, or sometimes 3, of the activities of daily living (ADLs).

The decision to buy LTCi is essentially a decision to cap the level of risk one is willing to take with their money and transfer the remaining risk to a third-party (that is the purpose of any type of insurance after all). LTCi policies are not one size fits all. There are a number of features to choose from when purchasing a policy, including the amount of daily or monthly coverage, elimination period (the amount of time you will pay for your own care before the coverage begins), number of years of coverage, inflation protection, and more. Additionally, there are a number of new "non-traditional" LTCi plans that are growing in popularity such as life insurance/ LTCi combination plans. When choosing a policy, be sure to work with an experienced and reputable agent or financial planner to help evaluate your choices and find a plan that is suitable for your unique situation.

The LTCI industry is rapidly changing. The combination of actuarial miscalculations and a low interest rate environment have caused many carriers to increase premiums and others to drop out of the business altogether. Yet, LTCi will always have its place among those who fall in the private pay category. A number of quality LTCi providers remain who have been in the business for a long time and who will continue to evolve and develop new products to better meet consumer needs. Additionally, many states are introducing new long-term care partnership programs to help encourage the purchase of long-term care insurance by those who are in position to pay for it. See the resources section of this book for more information on LTCi partnership programs.

The Relationship between Long-Term Care Insurance and CCRCs

As described earlier, residents of Full Service Retirement Communities that enter into Type-A (life-care) contracts will not face an increase in monthly charges when long-term care services are required, with the exception of pure inflationary adjustments or ancillary expenses. Therefore, some may ask the question of whether or not they should buy or maintain long-term care insurance if they enter into a Type-A contract.

Indeed, a Type-A contract functions like an insurance policy in the sense that a resident's out-of-pocket expenses are capped regardless of how much health care is needed. However, there are reasons why it is not a good idea to drop coverage if you already own it.

Quite often residents who enter into Type-A contracts are still able to use their LTCi. Suppose, for instance, that the continuing care contract only applies to care received in the on-site health care facility, but a resident decides they would like to hire a Home Health Care provider to come into their independent living unit for a few hours each day. In this case they would be required to pay out-of-pocket for these charges and they could potentially use LTCi to cover some or all of the cost.

Or, suppose a resident with a Type-A contract needs to move out of the community; perhaps they are not happy or there are extenuating circumstances. If this occurs and they move to another retirement community that requires residents to pay the full market rate for health care services then deciding to drop their LTCi may prove to be a regrettable decision.

CHAPTER 7

Conclusions

Aging is inevitable and your ability to remain able and independent throughout your lifetime is uncertain. However, your future care and comfort can be secure with proper planning and guidance. By anticipating your future needs and considering which retirement living alternative is best suited to address them, you and your family can approach your later years with confidence and peace of mind.

Moreover, planning is only becoming more important as the number of adult children available to "arrange, coordinate, provide and/or pay for long-term care services is expected to decline."[36]

According to the AARP Public Policy Institute, the ratio of family caregivers, defined as the number of potential family caregivers aged 45-64 for each person aged 80 or older, was 7:1 in 2010. This ratio is projected to fall to 4:1 by the year 2030 and 3:1 beyond that.[37] Thus, for many who are either in

---

36 Singletary, Michelle. "Long-term, Who Will Take Care of You?" *The Washington Post* 3 Sept. 2013. *The Washington Post* Web. 9 Sept. 2013.

37 D. Redfoot, L. Feinberg, A. Houser. "The Aging of the Baby Boom and the Growing Care Gap: A Look at Future Declines in the Availability of Family Caregivers." *AARP Public Policy Institute*, Aug. 2013. Web. 14 Dec. 2013.

or approaching the mid-retirement years this will make aging at home more difficult and likely more costly.

If you are in your mid-retirement years, NOW is the time to begin planning. If you have adult children consider having an open and honest discussion with them about your housing and care preferences for the later stages of life. If you seek to age at home then carefully consider each of the implications referenced in Chapter 2.

If, however, you determine that aging at home could be impractical, either due to lack of a family caregiver or for other reasons, then you need to consider the alternatives. Some of the challenges of aging at home could be addressed by simply downsizing, or by moving to an Active Adult Community or Senior Living Co-Op. Yet, these options do not provide the type of health care services you may eventually require. As described in Chapter 3, some people find peace of mind living in a retirement community that provides access to the types of health care services they may eventually require, although such communities often require a significant financial commitment, which may not be feasible for everyone.

For more information to help you make the choice that is best for you, please see the resources section provided in the back of this book. Congratulations on taking the first steps in planning for your future housing and health care needs!

Resources

- LifeSite Logics: www.MyLifeSite.net

- LeadingAge: www.leadingage.org

- National Continuing Care Residents Association (NaC-CRA): www.naccra.com

- American Seniors Housing Association: https://www.seniorshousing.org/index.php

- Continuing Care Accreditation Commission (Division of CARF): www.carf.org/Resources/RetirementLiving/

- *Today's Continuing Care Retirement Community*: https://www.seniorshousing.org/filephotos/research/CCRC_whitepaper.pdf

- Classifications for Seniors Housing Properties: https://www.seniorshousing.org/filephotos/Classifications_for_Seniors_Housing_Property_Types.pdf

- Naturally Occurring Retirement Communities (NORCS): http://www.norcs.org/

- Senior Cooperative Housing: http://seniorcoopliving.org/

- Book: *What's the Deal with Long-Term Care?* http://ltc.peopletested.com

- *Genworth Financial Cost of Care Study 2013*: https://www.genworth.com/corporate/about-genworth/industry-expertise/cost-of-care.html

- U.S. Dept. of Veterans Affiars- LTC benefits: www.va.gov/geriatrics/guide/longtermcare/

- U.S. Dept. of Health and Human Services: www.longtermcare.gov

- American Association of Long Term Care Insurance: www.aaltci.org

- Federal Long-Term Care Partnership Program: http://www.ltcfeds.com/index.html

- Merrill Lynch and AgeWave- *Americans' Perspectives on New Retirement Realities and the Longevity Bonus:* http://wealthmanagement.ml.com/publish/content/application/pdf/GWMOL/2013_Merrill_Lynch_Retirement_Study.pdf

- AARP Caregiving Resource Center: http://www.aarp.org/home-family/caregiving/

- National Alliance for Caregiving: http://www.caregiving.org/resources

- Book: *Having the Talk: The Four Keys to Your Parents' Safe Retirement* http://talk.peopletested.com

About the Author

Brad is co-founder of My LifeSite (formerly LifeSite Logics), a North Carolina company that develops web-based tools and resources designed to help families make better-informed decisions when considering a continuing care retirement community.

Brad previously spent thirteen years as a financial advisor before starting My LifeSite and still maintains the Certified Financial Planner™ certification. His extensive knowledge of the retirement living industry, combined with his financial planning background, allows him to provide valuable insights about lifestyle, healthcare, and financial planning considerations related to this significant life decision.

He's has been quoted in national media such as *Kiplinger's Magazine*, Wall Street Journal's *MarketWatch*, *USA Today* and the New York Times. He speaks regularly for retirement living providers, financial planners, industry trade organizations, life-long learning classes, and other groups across the country.

LifeSite Logics
Brad C. Breeding, CFP®, President
8354 Six Forks Rd. Suite 104
Raleigh, NC 27615
O: 919.848.6766
Website: www.MyLifeSite.net
Email: brad@mylifesite.net

CPSIA information can be obtained at www.ICGtesting.com
Printed in the USA
LVOW07s1807151015

458426LV00007B/122/P